Mimi's Family Recipes
a collection of Italian delicacies

written by
Marie B. Tavano

Copyright © 2014 Marie B. Tavano

All rights reserved.

ISBN: 1500831700
ISBN-13: 978-1500831707

for my girls
Michelle
Debra
Joy-Ann

Beef Stew

6 Idaho potatoes
4 carrots
1 large onion
1 can tomato sauce
oil
1 lb stew meat
1 bag frozen peas

Brown onion, stew meat and carrots in a large pan with oil. Cook until carrots are soft, then add tomato sauce. Let simmer for about 10 minutes. Add diced potatoes and mix well. Fill pan to the top. Cook until potatoes are soft. Add frozen peas. Cook additional 10 minutes.

Serve.

Breaded Steak

large piece Sirloin Steak ½ inch thick
3 eggs
¼ cup grated cheese
chopped parsley
garlic
salt
pepper
plain bread crumbs

Cut steak in to 4 square pieces. In a bowl mix eggs and grated cheese. Add parsley, garlic, salt and pepper. Dip steak in egg mixture and then in plain bread crumbs. In a large frying pan heat oil. Cook breaded steak about 2 minutes on each side.

Serve.

Chicken Cutlets

4 eggs
grated cheese
salt & pepper to taste
chicken cutlets
plain bread crumbs
oil

In a large bowl beat eggs, grated cheese, salt and pepper. Dip each chicken cutlet in the egg mixture and then in plain bread crumbs. In a large frying pan with oil, fry your chicken cutlets 3 minutes on each side. You may cover for a few minutes to make sure they are cooked.

Enjoy.

Mimi's Chicken Soup

1 whole chicken breast skin on
1 whole onion
2 stalks celery
3 carrots
1 can chicken broth
pastina

Fill a large pot with water. Add chicken, carrots, celery and onion. Boil for about 1 hour. Add chicken broth. In a separate pot bring water to a boil. Add pastina. Cook until tender. Add cooked pastina to soup.

Eggplant

1 large eggplant
8-10 eggs
½ cup grated cheese
2 cups flour
canola oil

Peel eggplant. Slice into thin slices. Set aside. In a large bowl, mix eggs and grated cheese, whisk with a fork until blended well. Place flour in separate bowl. Place eggplant slices in flour tossing eggplant to coat evenly. Dip floured eggplant pieces to egg and cheese mixture.
Heat oil in a frying pan. Cook coated eggplant slices in oil, turning when brown. Drain each slice on paper towel.

Serve plain or with gravy.

Escarole & Beans

1 head escarole
olive oil
cloves of garlic
salt and pepper
1 can white beans

Wash escarole in cold water to remove any dirt on the leaves. Cut escarole into small pieces. In a frying pan add olive oil and garlic. Cook escarole until tender. Add salt and pepper to taste. Add beans. Let simmer 5-10 minutes.

Enjoy.

Mimi's Holiday Stuffing

1 lb ground beef
1 lb sausage meat
1 bag Pepperidge farm herb stuffing
1 ½ cups milk
1 large onion
2 large Idaho potatoes boiled
1 stick butter
olive oil

Brown onion with ground beef and sausage. In a saucepan heat milk and add stuffing mix and ½ stick butter. Mix until stuffing cubes are very soft. In a large baking dish add onions, ground beef and sausage. Mix well. Add cubed boiled potatoes and add ½ stick butter. Mix well. Add a drizzle of olive oil and mix.

Bake at 350 degrees for 30 minutes.

Hot Dogs & Potatoes

2 tbsp corn oil
6 hot dogs (preferably Saugy)
4 Idaho potatoes cubed
salt and pepper
garlic powder

Cut hot dogs into one inch size pieces. Place in frying pan with oil. Add potatoes, salt, pepper and garlic. Cook until both potatoes and hot dogs are brown.

Enjoy!

Lasagna

10 lasagna noodles
1 tsp oil
ricotta
shredded mozarella
grated cheese
tomato sauce
small meatballs

Bring 8 cups of water to boil with oil so they won't stick together. Add lasagna noodles one at a time. Boil noodles for 8-10 minutes. In a 9x12 glass dish, line the bottom with a little gravy, enough to coat the bottom. Place 3 lasagna noodles on the bottom. Spoon ricotta onto noodles then spoon a little gravy and small meatballs atop the ricotta. Spread shredded mozzarella cheese and grated cheese over the gravy. Now it's time for the next layer of noodles. Do the same as you did with the first layer. Continue with layers until you have reached the top of the pan.

Bake at 350 degrees for 1 hour.

Italian Meatballs

8 eggs
3 tablespoons grated cheese
2 lbs 80% ground beef
plain bread crumbs

In a large bowl combine eggs and grated cheese. Wisk mixture well with a fork. Once blended, add 2 lbs ground beef, breaking up with fork to mix egg and grated cheese evenly. Add bread crumbs until it is firm enough to roll into meatballs. Roll meatballs approximately the size of a golf ball. Wetting your hands with cold water will help to roll the meatballs without sticking to your hands.

Meatballs can be fried in oil and garlic or cooked in hot gravy. To fry, cook until brown, turning throughout the cooking process. To cook in gravy, cook for 1 ½ hours on medium heat.

Enjoy!

Pasta & Beans

1 lb elbow macaroni
1 can cannelini white beans
2 small cans tomato sauce
1 clove garlic
2 tbsp corn oil

In a pot add oil, tomato sauce, garlic and beans. Simmer 10 minutes on low heat. In a another pot, add elbow macaroni to boiling water. When macaroni is tender, rinse under cold water. Add cooked macaroni to tomato sauce, garlic and beans. Top with grated cheese.

Enjoy!

Peppers & Sausage

5 red peppers
4 links sweet italian sausage
chopped garlic
salt and pepper to taste
parsley
corn oil
1 medium can tomato sauce (tuttoroso)
grated cheese

Wash peppers. Cut peppers into strips, removing seeds. Combine oil and peppers in pan. Mix well to coat peppers with oil. Cut sausage into approximately one inch pieces. Add to peppers and oil. Add salt, pepper, garlic and parsley.
Bake at 400 degrees for 30-45 minutes. Remove from oven, add tomato sauce. Mix well. Place back in oven for 15 minutes at 350 degrees. Remove from oven, place on top of stove and add grated cheese. Cover.

Enjoy!

Potatoes & Eggs

1 large onion cubed
2 large Idaho potatoes cubed (Idaho only !)
2 tbsp corn oil
6 – 8 eggs
salt and pepper to taste
chopped garlic
chopped parsley
1 tbsp grated cheese

Saute chopped onions, chopped potatoes, salt, pepper, parsley and garlic in a frying pan. Cook til potatoes are soft and brown. Beat eggs and grated cheese. Add egg and grated cheese mixture to frying pan. Lower heat. Cook til egg is pulling away from pan on sides, periodically pulling egg away from sides so raw egg runs underneath. Once egg is no longer runny, take a large dish that is larger than your frying pan. Place o top. With a gloved hand, flip the omelet onto the dish. Slide back into th frying pan and cook approximately 4-5 minutes on low heat. Remove from heat and let cool for a couple of minutes.
Enjoy!

Stuffed Peppers

6 red or green peppers
1 loaf stale Italian bread
½ cup grated cheese
1 can chopped black olives
1 cup dry sausage or capicola
parsley
1 can tomato sauce
olive oil

Cut Italian bread into bite size cubes. Combine all ingredients except the peppers in a large bowl. Mix well with your hands til mixture is a mushy consistency. Cut tops off peppers and remove seeds from inside. Spoon mixture into each pepper. Place in baking dish covering each pepper with a drizzle of olive oil.

Bake at 350 for 1 hour.

Tomatoes & Eggs

2 tbsp corn oil
1 small can tomato sauce
5 eggs
salt and pepper
garlic powder
grated cheese

In a frying pan with oil put tomato sauce. Season with garlic powder. Simmer for 5 minutes on medium heat. Beat eggs. Add eggs to tomato sauce. Mix occasionally as if cooking scrambled eggs. Top with grated cheese when serving.

Enjoy.

Tortellini, Peas & Ham

1 ham steak cubed
1 box frozen peas
1 package tortellini - cheese or meat
1 jar alfredo sauce
2 tbsp corn oil
salt and pepper
garlic powder

In a frying pan with oil saute ham and peas. Add garlic powder, salt and pepper. Add tortellini to boiling water until soft. Add tortellini to ham and peas. Stir together and add alfredo sauce. Simmer for 5 minutes.

Enjoy!

Veal Parmigiana

6 pieces veal cutlet
4 eggs
2 tbsp grated cheese
3 tbsp corn oil
plain bread crumbs
2 cups Italian gravy
1 bag shredded mozarella cheese
salt and pepper

Beat eggs together with grated cheese. Dip veal cutlet one by one into egg mixtur then into breadcrumbs. In a large frying pan with oil cook each cutlet 2-3 minutes per side. Place on paper towel to drain off oil. Then place in baking dish covering each cutlet with gravy, mozarella cheese and grated cheese. Salt and pepper to taste. Bake at 350 degree until cheese melts 15-20 minutes.

Enjoy!

Veal, Peas & Mushrooms

2 tbsp corn oil
1 package frozen peas
1 lb veal stew meat
2 small cans mushrooms
2 cloves garlic

Place veal in frying pan with oil. Stirring periodically until veal is brown on all sides. Add peas, garlic. Cook for a couple of minutes. Add mushrooms. Cover for 15 minutes over low heat.

Serve.

Rice Pie

1 ½ cups rice (not instant!)
12 eggs
1 ½ cups sugar
1 small container heavy cream
1 quart whole milk
1 large container Ricotta (preferably Supreme)
nutmeg
Pilsbury pie crust pre made

Boil rice. Set aside.
In a 9 x 12 glass baking dish, place crust on bottom and sides. Crimp edges. Set aside.
In a large bowl, beat eggs and mix well with sugar. Add heavy cream, milk and ricotta. Stir well. Ladle mixture of eggs, milk, heavy cream, sugar and ricotta into pie crust. Approximately 6 tablespoons. Be careful not to overfill. Sprinkle top with nutmeg.
Bake at 325 degrees for 1 ½ hours or until golden brown on top. Let cool. Cut into squares and serve.

Gravy

2 large cans crushed tomato
1 can tomato paste
1 can tomato Sauce
1 can water (crushed tomato can)
basil
black Pepper

Combine crushed tomato, tomato paste, tomato sauce, water, basil and black pepper in a large pot. Cook on low for 2 hours.

Enjoy!

Made in the USA
Columbia, SC
27 August 2022